twenty

m montalbano

Publisher: michael montalbano
2020

First Printing: 2020

ISBN 978-1-716-58463-3

Michael Montalbano
Penfield NY 14526

Printed in the United States of America

cover art, 'larkins aubade' by m montalbano

these are dark times

and yet

an admonition

for those who are broken spirited

and road weary

no more seven days

rise

moments at rest

contents of mind languidly surface

ripples

on a stilled pond

a cloud of clarity

liberated from influence

and overhearing

noiseless

illumed

nothingness

peacefulness

an opportunity to filter the prevailing culture

animal mind

a silent contemplation of the world beyond words

this bold red dog

and i not i

sense the trap

of philosophical boasts,

the trick of tropes

and obfuscation

and treachery

on religion

alas, the cloven hoof

sends people through the roof

and i, aloof

require a different proof

the bold satanic trotter

not cleansed by holy watter

and i, the rotter

eat bacon like i otter

an

arrant midnight upon

this hostile island of

dying moons and

salted wounds

grounded glass and

fists thrust in eyes

this moribund country

built upon the blood of others

to grasp

the toxicity of the gatekeepers

upon this bittered land

is not to suggest they cannot be moved

they can be moved profoundly

projecting malfeasance upon the other

with cowardly rolls at the roulette table

at odds with the house

on ethics

on civility

that one could grasp the origins

in this most advantageous of hotels

the blame lies solely upon the feet

of the usual suspects

with wagers of

degraded discourse

and heavy-slurred speech

and the eminence grise croupiers

giving hand signals

before the wheel is spun

crowd

consorting with cylindrical uprights

crowing with the crowd

cavorting with monied practices

shameless

fatuous socialites supplanting authority

duplicitous decisions

specious sage judgements

altering destinies to meet the need

for fame

lawlessness

movers and shakers

deciding what must be done

to build their better world,

with raucous celebrations,

feasts in your own backyard

insanity

a poorly drawn rule

or an ill-defined edict

is a sieve

for the ambitious,

who would foment fear for their cause,

lining their pockets with the dripping gold

amidst the chaos

the moral inequities

and unfettered deceptions,

an additional burden that

once an idea enters the world,

though it may be re-shaped or advanced,

it will never exit,

strung along by the skilled men

of letters and words

who can be of disreputable character

and all the while

these statesmen

are shifting their weight

over unsettled graves

it is unnatural to become indifferent to these types of solicitations

the elderly neighbor

who cannot remember

the wife

confused in remembering him

the sickness

they hold on to

they sleep

this nightmare

this painful end of breath

beyond unopened doors and shuttered sheets

do we

ignore, abhor them?

something in each of us dies these days

for what we have been compelled to refuse

to hold suffering

at arm's length

without dignity

proper ornamentation

placed upon a shelf

as old books in a row

clear lack of meaning

but for the claws of the church

this unwieldy burden

this complex human world

we now know

virus

a blackened sun

in a formidable sky

yields unbalanced forces

upon the ground

and shifting plates

beneath the feet

boundaryless

with open eyes

or forever sleep

all will be humbled

there is talk of war

there is talk of defiance and risk

and while this disease is mercurial

distilled disquisition on many things

with raised eyebrows and clenching fists

our brother leon knew this well

that battle must needs come from within

and infected blood will be spilled or drained

as we continue to mourn this pain

this large quiet time

stilled, against the grain

"there will be no dancing on a wall during this mad dysfunctional kingship"
--j meacham

presidential

the worm is at work

laboriously boring wholes

deep in the groundswell

halves

in the countryside

tunnels

in the vision

with notions of

shudders and pleasures

dirt and grift

leaving behind

trails of slime

and ingratitude

flat land

the intractability of

a single view from the field

stomping out brushfires

the man constructed dogs of straw

around his property

to keep the wolves at bay

and thoughts

pounding fence posts in the ground

of 'superior' virtue

and whether

violence is a tool

or a therapeutic

ellipses

upon well-trodden paths

engaged in a gathering of

food for the tribe

only to return

to the nest

empty handed

sojourn

the wandering instinct

satisfied through curiosity

and emergence from

a deliquescent past

beyond immovable oceans and plains

i did not choose this path

it was thrust upon me

if i sit too long i loathe

i shudder

at this aberration

some have chosen

to call leader,

their guide through backwater

having no authority

to chronicle

compels one to come to terms with

roiling masses of peoples

lawless arrogance and empathetic pride

enveloped in the opacity

of acrid smoke and tears that blind the eye

journals see what they see

robe's beer, from the pot

a man did speak to me one time

of killing kings with vacuous rhyme

i held his feet to flame and said

'but why not simply lop off head?'

winter

is coming

those above the snow line

are well prepared

others

will suffer

caught unawares

by their own antipathies

to reason

the purposeless snow

centuries

artifacts

earthen vessels

carved and impervious

marked, symbolled

empty clay

shaped

ported

filled at the river

the essence of pearls

silken, milky opacity

an old womans eye

a young girls dream

a string for forgiveness

a ring for a delicate lobe

gem of the sea

from the depths

from nothingness

a monarch emerges

a damaged wing

a larva

feeding, feeding

sleeping in the warmth

of a lone cocoon

sheltered, protected

this worm-like phase

to burst forth

from its white house

with fiery vigor

witless

beneath a reddening sun

flitting about

without purpose

but to feed

with tube-like tongue

ephemeral beauty

ephemeral ambulation

for its dulled audience

tempest

ariadne's cries

vast seething seas of change

punishing windstorms

stark cleansing rains

dark crumbling shorelines

uprooted claims

devastation

reconstruction

hope

a comfortable hole

warm and

all-embracing

a fire flows,

an eye thread of light

the mercury runs,

and i wed my soul

reflections

in an obsidian mirror

twenty

there is not time

to walk among the dead

the quiet field is filled

with those who will not speak

there is not time

to tolerate intolerables

to reflect upon origins

to accept

this indecent indifference to a life

i will not wait

for diseased minds to cry hoax

i, too

have miles to go

the stench of death and politics

sickens me

and i would shun

my misanthropic ways

but for the boisterous bedlam

and lawless orgy

a turn of the heel

to the canvas

and library

and solace